Careers in Environmental and Energy Technology

Other titles in the *High-Tech Careers* series include:

Careers in Gaming
Careers in Internet Technology
Careers in Medical Technology
Careers in Robotics

Careers in Environmental and Energy Technology

John Allen

ReferencePoint Press®

© 2017 ReferencePoint Press, Inc.
Printed in the United States

For more information, contact:
ReferencePoint Press, Inc.
PO Box 27779
San Diego, CA 92198
www.ReferencePointPress.com

LIBRARY OF CONGRESS CATALOGING-IN-PUBLICATION DATA

Names: Allen, John, 1957- author.
Title: Careers in environmental and energy technology / by John Allen.
Description: San Diego, CA : ReferencePoint Press, Inc., 2017. | Series: High-tech careers | Includes bibliographical references and index.
Identifiers: LCCN 2016033948 (print) | LCCN 2016038217 (ebook) | ISBN 9781682821107 (hardback) | ISBN 9781682821114 (eBook)
Subjects: LCSH: Environmental engineering--Vocational guidance--Juvenile literature. | Energy industries--Vocational guidance--Juvenile literature.
Classification: LCC TD156 .A45 2017 (print) | LCC TD156 (ebook) | DDC 621.042023--dc23
LC record available at https://lccn.loc.gov/2016033948

Contents

Introduction: High-Tech Jobs That Improve
the Environment   6

Environmental Analyst   10

Solar PV Installer   18

Wind Turbine Technician   26

Energy Consultant   33

Air Quality Forecaster   40

Petroleum Engineer   47

Fuel Cell Engineer   54

Renewable Energy Project Developer   61

Interview with a Renewable Energy Project
Developer   68

Other Jobs in Environmental and Energy
Technology   71

Index   72

Picture Credits   79

About the Author   80

High-Tech Jobs That Improve the Environment

In June 2016 Tesla Motors, a maker of electric-powered automobiles, made an offer to buy SolarCity, which designs and installs residential rooftop solar panels. Elon Musk, Tesla's cofounder and chief executive officer, saw the proposed merger as a perfect synergy of green technologies—a combination that produces a bigger bang than the sum of its individual parts. Musk, who also helped found SolarCity and is a large stockholder, envisions a home in the future where solar panels on the roof transfer power to a wall-mounted battery in the garage, which in turn recharges the electric car in the driveway. "This would start with the car that you drive and the energy that you use to charge it," Tesla announced on its company blog, "and would extend to how everything else in your home or business is powered." Musk promotes this vision as the perfect example of energy technology that is practical, efficient, and environmentally friendly. For the nearly forty-five thousand employees at the two companies, from energy storage specialists and solar energy system engineers to information technology experts and sales personnel, cutting-edge technology is helping to provide good jobs that also improve the environment.

High-Tech Solutions to Energy Needs

Protecting the environment and using resources wisely are important goals today in both the public and private sectors. Governments at all levels, large corporations, and smaller companies are all seeking high-tech solutions to meet the world's energy needs in ways that are clean and sustainable. The rapid growth of this so-called green industry promises to create new jobs and careers for decades to come. Driving this growth are exciting new technologies related to alternative energy and the pursuit of clean air and water.

According to the International Renewable Energy Agency (IRENA), in 2015 green energy jobs in the United States increased by 6 percent to almost 222,000, surpassing the total from the slumping oil and gas industry. "The continued growth in the renewable energy sector is significant because it stands in contrast to trends across the energy sector," Adnan Z. Amin, director general of IRENA, says on the agency's website. Worldwide, jobs in alternative energy increased by 5 percent in 2015. More than 8 million workers were employed in solar, wind, and other renewable energy sectors. IRENA forecasts that by 2030 the number of clean energy jobs in the world will reach 24 million.

A good deal of the job growth in green energy comes from government incentive programs and special financing plans. Even well-known companies like Tesla often depend on government subsidies of various kinds. Yet spending on green technology also provides plenty of excellent job opportunities, judging by the factors of wages, job growth, and job openings nationwide. These jobs range from traditional occupations that are well suited to green objectives to new careers made possible by technological breakthroughs.

For example, jobs for electricians are expected to grow by about 12 percent in the next decade, helped by the fact that electrical work is necessary to connect solar panels and wind turbines to the power grid. Carpenters are needed to reinforce roofs for solar panel installations and to modify houses and businesses to use energy more efficiently. Geologists and geoscientists, highly paid professions slated to grow by 18 percent, search not only for oil and gas deposits but also for geothermal springs as a source of clean energy. Large solar arrays and wind turbine farms provide jobs for engineers and technicians that did not exist only a short time ago. Fuel cell engineers, materials scientists, and chemists are working on new technologies that may completely change the way our society uses energy. One day many homes and businesses may be powered by energy from ocean tides, space-based solar panels, or microscopic bacteria linked to electrodes.

Careers in Environmental and Energy Technology

Occupation	Entry-Level Education	2015 Median Pay
Electricians	High school diploma or equivalent	$51,880
Environmental Engineering Technicians	Associate's degree	$48,650
Environmental Engineers	Bachelor's degree	$84,560
Environmental Science and Protection Technicians	Associate's degree	$43,030
Environmental Scientists and Specialists	Bachelor's degree	$67,460
Geoscientists	Bachelor's degree	$89,700
Hydrologists	Bachelor's degree	$79,550
Nuclear Engineers	Bachelor's degree	$102,950
Nuclear Technicians	Associate's degree	$80,260
Power Plant Operators, Distributors, and Dispatchers	High school diploma or equivalent	$75,660
Solar Photovoltaic Installers	High school diploma or equivalent	$37,830
Wind Turbine Technicians	Some college, no degree	$51,050

Bureau of Labor Statistics, *Occupational Outlook Handbook*, 2016. www.bls.gov/ooh.

A Variety of Careers and Jobs

Working with the environment and alternative energy affords the choice of a wide variety of careers and jobs. Students interested in this field can study to become an air quality forecaster, aquatic biologist, energy consultant, nuclear engineer, turf scientist, soil conservation technician, wind turbine technician, solar engineer, landscape designer, wetlands specialist, solar panel installer, or environmental analyst, among dozens of other rewarding careers. Many of these positions require a background in science, mathematics, or computers, and most call for an undergraduate degree plus on-the-job training. They also offer exciting opportunities for travel, meeting people, and working with like-minded colleagues on fascinating projects. High-tech environmental and energy-related jobs tend to be well paid, particularly those that involve engineering or scientific research. Surveys also show that workers in this industry report very high levels of job satisfaction. A recent global survey by the Institute of Environmental Management & Assessment found that more than 80 percent of those whose jobs are in environmental professions or sustainability label themselves as generally happy in their work and satisfied with their salaries.

Using technology to help solve the world's problems of energy use and pollution can be very rewarding work. Students who study to enter this field likely will find a ready market for their skills. They also will discover great opportunities for a satisfying career. "Purpose doesn't have to be your primary driver," notes Nic Stover, former chief executive officer at Calcom Solar and Polaris Energy Services, on the website Environmental Science.org. "But I do believe that a sustainable industry like renewable energy allows people to combine passion, mission, profession, and vocation into something they love, something they are great at, something the world needs, and ultimately, something you get paid for!"

Environmental Analyst

What Does an Environmental Analyst Do?

In private companies and at every level of government, the focus on environmental issues has never been greater. With the ability to analyze these issues and design practical solutions, the environmental analyst offers a crucial service. He or she employs the latest technology and scientific methods to collect data about a specific problem, such as soil use, water pollution, or the effect of factory emissions on air quality. Using knowledge of statistics, mathematics, and cutting-edge technology, the environmental analyst will design a model for solving the problem and recommend the best methods to put the plan into effect. Besides scientific expertise, he or she must also have the ability to work with a team and communicate clearly. A successful environmental analyst is equally at ease in the office and laboratory, out in the field, and in the corporate boardroom or government agency meeting.

At a Glance:
Environmental Analyst

Minimum Educational Requirements
Bachelor's degree, usually in environmental science

Personal Qualities
Strong communication and teamwork skills; detail oriented

Valuable Skills
Data analysis; digital mapping; computer modeling; familiarity with geographic information systems

Working Conditions
Office work with some outdoor fieldwork

Salary Range
About $40,350 to $118,070

Number of Jobs
As of 2014 about 94,600

Future Job Outlook
Growth rate of 11 percent through 2024

Environmental analysts typically work with government regulations that strive to ensure clean air, safe water, and soil free from hazardous materials. Government agencies use environmental analysts to help them develop laws and regulations that protect the environment. Companies in the private sector need environmental analysts to make sure that they are complying with these laws. Green organizations hire environmental analysts to help them craft lobbying campaigns for new regulations. In each job the analyst uses data to draft or carry out a plan of action. One example from the government side is an analyst who works to protect water resources for the New England Interstate Water Pollution Control Commission. He describes his duties on JustJobs.com: "What my job entails is to provide technical support and the implementation of regulations as well as regional guidance on program activity. It is my job to keep up with all regulatory matters concerning drinking water, water supply, groundwater, water protection and climate change issues." This analyst uses computer technology to stay current with the dizzying array of water regulations that cover the New England states and federal lands.

Environmental analysts in both government and the private sector often develop response plans to potential disasters such as floods, hurricanes, landslides, wildfires, oil spills, and the release of chemicals. These scientists project the possible impact on an area's wildlife, soil, air, and waterways and groundwater, among other aspects. An environmental analyst may also be called on to answer questions or provide background facts following a high-profile disaster. After the 2010 BP oil spill in the Gulf of Mexico, energy companies increasingly sought out environmental analysts to do detailed risk assessments for future deepwater oil rigs in the gulf and other offshore sites.

Firms also use environmental analysts to perform environmental site assessments for business or factory sites and their surroundings. Assessment is done before construction begins, continues while the site is in use, and is performed again when the site is about to be abandoned. Here an analyst might monitor the use and storage of hazardous materials, regularly test soil and water samples in the area, test for emissions, and ensure compliance with all the appropriate laws and regulations with regard to local ecosystems and resources.

The main job of an environmental analyst is research. He or she

An environmental analyst obtains a water sample for testing. In addition to evaluating water, soil, or air quality, such analysts provide technical support for development of environmental laws and making sure companies adhere to them.

first creates a plan for data collection to suit the research project. Then the analyst goes into the field to collect samples of air, soil, plants, and water to test for pollution levels. He or she also compares and interprets historical data for the particular area being studied. Once fieldwork is completed, the worker enters the laboratory to analyze samples with the most precise, cutting-edge technology. For example, one tool is mass spectrometry, which is used to find contaminants in wastewater. The sample is bombarded with electrons, causing its molecules to be ionized, or broken into charged fragments. These ions are then sorted according to their mass-to-charge ratio. This allows the analyst to identify pollutants at the molecular level. Another tool is gas chromatography. This moves a sample, either gas or a vaporized liquid, through an air stream that leads into a specially packed tube. The tube separates the sample into its component substances, which can then be identified by a detector. Gas chromatography is often used as a rapid test for emissions such as nitrogen dioxide and carbon dioxide.

When the lab work is finished, the environmental analyst must study and interpret the data. The analyst uses the data in digitized form to create tables, charts, graphs, and reports that summarize the findings. He or she is then ready to make recommendations to a board, committee, or client. This guidance is used to make policy decisions. The analyst might also use the data to provide expert testimony to a government agency or in a court proceeding.

There are plenty of opportunities for an environmental analyst to specialize. For example, a climate change analyst focuses on how ecosystems are affected by an altered climate. An industrial ecologist works with clients such as mining operators and manufacturers to limit adverse effects on the environment and weigh the costs and benefits of certain measures. An environmental health specialist studies risks to human health from contamination of the air, water, or soil. A site restoration planner examines a polluted site and designs a plan to clean it up. Environmental analysts may also become teachers in high schools or postsecondary institutions.

How Do You Become an Environmental Analyst?

Education

Entry-level jobs for an environmental analyst in government or the private sector usually require only a bachelor's degree in environmental science or a science-related field. Certain schools offer a specific degree in environmental analysis. Most colleges and universities in the United States offer some sort of environmental studies program, and many help students customize their course load to meet certain career goals. To get an undergraduate degree in environmental science, a student might take courses in biology, chemistry, soil science, forestry, plant and animal physiology, hazardous waste management, environmental law, and statistics. Courses tend to require a significant amount of fieldwork and laboratory time for valuable hands-on experience. A student might serve an internship to get on-the-job training. It can also be helpful to take a writing course that includes technical writing.

Most employers prefer candidates with a master's degree in environmental science, and some consider it essential for advancement in the field. Studies in a master's degree program might range from hydrology and regulatory risk analysis to quantitative problem solving. Master's candidates may also be required to deliver a thesis based on original research or complete a project in environmental science. Those who seek a doctoral degree often benefit from specializing in one area, such as hydrology or chemistry. Such candidates usually plan to pursue an academic career or do independent research.

Certification and Continuing Education

Employers may require an environmental analyst to be certified as a professional in the field. The Academy of Board Certified Environmental Professionals affirms that a person with certain qualifications of education and experience is maintaining his or her expertise. Each year certified environmental professionals must complete forty hours of professional credit to keep their certification. The credit includes twenty hours earned for full-time employment as an environmental analyst and twenty hours of attendance at seminars, conferences, and continuing education classes. Some environmental analysts may have to become certified as specialists in their chosen field. For example, the Institute of Hazardous Materials Management certifies that a person is keeping up with developments related to hazardous materials and their disposal.

Internships

Some companies offer internships to aspiring environmental analysts. Often these jobs involve checking compliance with laws and regulations associated with new or ongoing projects. Energy Resources USA advertised for an intern at a salary of ten dollars an hour. The company's ad on the website jobspider.com said, "The individual must possess the ability to associate and communicate with a wide variety of people with tact, courtesy and professionalism. While this internship is largely about supporting the environmental areas, equally important is the expectation for the selected candidate to gain exposure and experience in an opportunity rich industry."

Skills and Personality

Employers seeking an environmental analyst look for qualities such as self-discipline, the ability to solve problems, and skill in communicating. Environmental analysts must be able to motivate themselves to work alone performing long hours of lab work or computer statistical analysis. At the same time, they must be comfortable working as a team with engineers and technicians in the field in gathering data. Employers value strong writing and speaking skills. Environmental analysts must present the results of their research clearly and concisely, in language that nonexperts can understand. It helps to be current with the latest technologies in data analysis, digital mapping, and computer modeling. Analysts should also be well versed in geographic information system software, which helps to store, manage, and present complex geographical data.

An environmental analyst must be passionate about environmental issues and the search for ways to protect the earth and use resources wisely. The ability to find practical solutions to problems is highly valued. A person who can avoid becoming frustrated by long work hours and temporary setbacks while maintaining a positive out look has the best chance of success in this field.

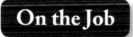

On the Job

Employers

An environmental analyst has the choice of many different employers and industries. Among the possibilities are private companies, such as Wyle Laboratories, which provides engineering and other technical services to the aerospace industry; federal, state, and local government agencies; environmental groups; consulting firms; colleges and universities; and research institutes. An analyst with a track record of success might be able to start his or her own independent consulting firm. Teaching or doing research can be fulfilling work for many analysts.

Working Conditions

An environmental analyst usually splits time between fieldwork and work inside an office or laboratory. Working outdoors may involve physically challenging travel and labor, with long, irregular hours in harsh conditions and remote locales. Sometimes there are dangers from collecting samples of pollutants or working in contaminated areas. Office and lab work calls for long hours and very detailed labor with statistics. Deadlines for preparing a presentation may increase job tensions.

Earnings

According to a May 2014 report by the US Bureau of Labor Statistics (BLS), the federal government paid environmental scientists and specialists an annual mean salary of $98,830. Analysts for local governments averaged $64,760, and those employed by states averaged $60,460. The top 10 percent of environmental analysts nationwide make about $114,990 a year, and the lowest 10 percent earn less than $40,350. The top five best-paying areas for this job are the District of Columbia, Virginia, California, Illinois, and Colorado.

What Is the Future Outlook for Environmental Analysts?

According to the BLS, employment opportunities in environmental analysis will grow 11 percent by 2024, which equates to more than ten thousand new jobs. Minimizing environmental damage and assessing impact will continue to be a major concern for government agencies and private firms in the future. The ability to design or assist in developing work sites, utilities, factories, and transportation systems that are in harmony with the surrounding ecosystem will assure the environmental analyst of being a valued employee for many years to come.

Find Out More

Association of Environmental Studies and Sciences (AESS)
website: www.aess.info

The AESS serves to connect the many environmental programs in North America and around the world. It provides environmental analysts and scientists with blogs and other information about continuing education and professional networking opportunities. The AESS publishes the *Journal of Environmental Studies and Sciences*.

Ecological Society of America (ESA)
website: www.esa.org

A nonprofit, nonpartisan group of scientists founded in 1915, the ESA promotes ecological science by facilitating communication among ecologists, environmental analysts and other professionals, and policy makers. The ESA website provides valuable information about career opportunities for environmental analysts and related specialists.

International Society for Industrial Ecology (ISIE)
website: www.is4ie.org

The ISIE provides a forum for natural and social scientists, engineers, policy makers, and other environmental professionals to share the latest methods, tools, and solutions in pursuit of sustainable technologies. The ISIE website includes job postings and other information for environmental analysts working with industrial ecology worldwide.

National Association of Environmental Professionals (NAEP)
website: www.naep.org

The NAEP connects professionals dedicated to advancing environmental professions. Its website provides a network of contacts for environmental analysts and current information on planning, technology, and research for environmental professionals.

Solar PV Installer

What Does a Solar PV Installer Do?

Harnessing the sun's energy to create electricity is one of today's most promising technologies for clean energy. Arrays of distinctive blue solar panels are a common sight on rooftops of commercial buildings and private homes. Homeowners are increasingly turning to solar panel technology to fulfill all their energy needs or supplement their energy use. According to a June 2016 report in *Fortune* magazine, solar technology is on the verge of becoming "ridiculously cheap." The report notes, "The low cost of solar will encourage solar panel installations to the point that solar could account for 43% of all the new power generation added worldwide between now and 2040." A solar photovoltaic (PV) installer sets up these solar panels on roofs and other structures. This worker installs solar panels according to building codes and community standards. He or she may work alone on some jobs, but typically a team is needed to perform an installation. Beginning installers build and mount frames and

---

At a Glance:
Solar PV Installer

Minimum Educational Requirements
High school diploma or vocational degree

Personal Qualities
Reliable; detail oriented; able to work with others; professional attitude with customers

Valuable Skills
Mechanical skills; facility with tools; ability to follow complex instructions; physical fitness and stamina

Working Conditions
Outdoors in all weather conditions; on ladders and rooftops

Salary Range
About $27,540 to $56,670

Number of Jobs
As of 2014 about 5,900

Future Job Outlook
Growth rate of 24 percent through 2024

support structures that position PV panels toward the sun. Then they install solar panels within or on top of these structures. More complicated tasks, such as hooking up electrical components or connecting the array of panels to the power grid, are often reserved for more experienced installers.

The job of a solar PV installer is not limited to installations atop commercial buildings or homes. An installer might help set up a large array of panels in the desert adjacent to a military base or factory. He or she might check and replace damaged PV panels on a solar farm project. The installer might evaluate and reinforce a stand-alone structure such as a barn or carport to ensure that it can bear the weight of several PV panels. Sometimes installers attach solar panels to poles or specially built towers. Once panels are installed, the worker might weatherproof them with sealants and protective metal flashing to prevent leaks. Whatever the job, a PV installer will benefit from having skills connected to construction work, especially roofing and framing. He or she must be expert at using appropriate hand tools (such as a crescent wrench, hammer, screwdriver, and pliers) and power tools (such as impact wrenches and drills). An installer must be comfortable working long hours on ladders and at great heights in weather conditions that are frequently harsh. Experience working with electrical wiring is also helpful, although in many states and localities only a licensed electrician can connect arrays of solar panels to the power grid.

Teams of experienced installers generally split up the tasks on a project to speed the job along. An installer who works quickly and efficiently is highly valued on such a crew. Usually installing the solar panels is put off until the very last step. As installer Kristin Underwood explains on the environmental site treehugger.com:

> This means that we can still tweak things on the roof up until the last minute and also minimizes the chance that we will get shocked either up on the roof or down below. Why? Well, as soon as sun hits the panels, they are producing energy. String a few panels together and you can pack quite a punch. So instead, we tend to do all the wiring, put the breaker into the main panel and close all the connections on the roof, and then put

the panels onto the system. That way when the panels hook together, the system is wired all the way to the service and there is no way to shock yourself.

The lead installer on a crew—who is typically a licensed electrician—checks to see that the finished system is activated and functioning properly. The system must be checked for correct wiring, polarity (ensuring wires are appropriately marked for positive or negative charge), and proper grounding. As solar installations increase, PV installers have more opportunities to work on checking existing systems and doing routine maintenance. Cleaning solar panels, replacing sealant, and checking wiring helps ensure that a system is operating efficiently and providing the greatest possible amount of electric power.

How Do You Become a Solar PV Installer?

Education

There are several ways to enter the growing field of solar panel installation. A beginning solar PV installer may have only a high school diploma. This type of worker can receive up to one year of on-the-job training working with crews of experienced installers. Another beginner may take a course at a technical school or community college before finding a job as an installer. Reacting to the growth of solar power, some large construction and roofing companies now operate apprentice programs to help candidates learn how to install and check solar panel systems. There are also detailed online training courses in solar installation. These courses are especially suitable for those who already have experience in related construction work, such as electricians and framers. "As the field takes off and as more and more funding goes into solar, companies will need a way to differentiate between candidates," says Underwood. "So, having a little experience and/or education under your tool belt wouldn't hurt."

Some solar panel manufacturers offer training on how to install specific new products. This training ensures that workers learn the correct installation techniques to maximize a product's potential. Solar companies also provide safety training for all of their installers.

Solar PV installers measure placement of rooftop solar panels. The job can include building and mounting frames and support structures, installing the panels, and connecting them to the power grid.

Certification

There is no mandatory certification for solar PV installers. However, certain professional groups certify installers on a voluntary basis to affirm their knowledge and expertise for potential employers. In general, a solar PV installer should have a working knowledge of different types of PV panels and the semiconductor materials used in them—materials ranging from silicon to carbon polymers.

The main source of certification for solar PV installers is the North American Board of Certified Energy Practitioners (NABCEP). To be certified by the NABCEP, installers (including PV project managers, system designers, and supervisors) must finish at least fifty-eight hours of advanced training in PV installation at an authorized school or organization. Each applicant must also take a ten-hour course in construction and workplace safety sponsored by the Occupational Safety & Health Administration. In addition, the applicant must pass a special exam and offer documented proof (system information, permits, inspections) of having completed three to five PV installation projects. Online practice exams are available to help applicants become comfortable with the format of the exam. Another organization that offers certification for PV installers is the Electronics Technicians Association, International. A group called Roof Integrated Solar Energy accredits installers with at least forty hours of education or training as certified solar roofing professionals. These workers must also have three years' experience in PV installation or roofing and have brought at least five PV installations to completion.

Skills and Personality

A successful PV installer must be good at working with a team and following instructions. He or she must be focused and detail oriented, as mistakes can lead to a solar panel system not working properly or even to injuries from electrical problems. Mechanical skills with a variety of tools and devices are essential to the PV installer in his or her work with complicated electrical equipment. Carpentry ability is needed to shore up rooftops and other structures to bear the weight of a solar panel system. An installer must also possess good people skills for dealing with residential and commercial customers. Personal responsibility and a strong work ethic ensure that the installer does what is necessary to get to jobs on time and meet deadlines.

On the Job

Employers

According to the US Bureau of Labor Statistics (BLS), 39 percent of solar PV installers worked for plumbing, heating, and air-conditioning firms in 2014, the largest percentage for any industry.

About 24 percent worked for electrical contractors. About 6 percent worked in construction related to power lines and connected structures. Solar companies are increasingly creating solar farms with vast arrays of panels and modules installed over a large area of ground, such as a desert or field. Installers are needed to build these farms and to test and maintain the panels once the project is completed. Solar Ready Vets, a joint effort of the US Department of Energy and the Department of Defense that began in 2014, also works to find US military veterans jobs as PV installers for the solar industry.

Working Conditions

PV installation is full-time work, and may include working on evenings and weekends to meet deadlines. This can be a difficult line of work for a person with a family. A solar PV installer often must be able to travel at a moment's notice. As solar energy companies fan out into new areas, jobs may be farther apart and require more travel time and days spent living out of a suitcase. In the summer, work often commences early in the morning and may extend to evening hours to avoid the most intense heat of the day.

Installers must have the physical strength to lift panels that can weigh as much as 50 pounds (23 kg), not to mention other heavy parts and equipment. Stamina is necessary to climb ladders, perch in awkward positions, and work for long hours in direct sunlight or in cramped areas such as attics and crawl spaces. There is always the risk of falling from a roof or a ladder as well as danger from electrical shocks and serious burns from hot panels and equipment. Safety precautions must be observed without fail.

Earnings

The BLS reported that the median annual wage for solar PV installers in 2014 was $37,830. Electrical contractors and other wiring contractors paid the top median annual wage at $39,150. The upper 10 percent of solar installers earned more than $56,670, and the lowest 10 percent earned about $27,540. The top five best-paying states for installers are Hawaii, New Jersey, Massachusetts, Colorado, and California.

What Is the Future Outlook for Solar PV Installers?

According to the BLS, the job outlook for solar PV installers is positive, although the occupation remains limited in size overall. Through 2024, the number of jobs is projected to grow by 24 percent, which is much faster than the average rate of growth. However, in raw numbers, this would result in only about fourteen hundred additional jobs. Should prices for solar panels continue to fall, it is likely that many homeowners will have systems installed. Government incentives such as subsidies and tax rebates for solar usage could also increase the industry's growth, providing more opportunities for installers in states committed to alternative energy.

Find Out More

Electrical Training Alliance
website: www.electricaltrainingalliance.org

The Electrical Training Alliance offers apprenticeship training especially for solar PV installers. The group is a joint training program between the National Electrical Contractors Association and the International Brotherhood of Electrical Workers. For years it has concentrated on training the best electrical workers in the industry.

Electronics Technicians Association, International (ETA)
website: www.eta-i.org

The ETA provides certification to installers who have received hands-on training from an ETA-approved school and have shown themselves to be knowledgeable in all aspects of solar panel installation, including troubleshooting methods and best safety practices.

National Center for Construction Education and Research (NCCER)
website: www.nccer.org

The NCCER was developed by construction industry CEOs and academic leaders to revolutionize training for the construction field. For solar PV workers, it provides curriculum materials for entry-level and advanced installation work. Its curriculum covers an introduction to solar photovol-taics, system design, and system installation.

North American Board of Certified Energy Practitioners (NABCEP)
56 Clifton Country Rd., Suite 202
Clifton Park, NY 12065
website: www.nabcep.org

The NABCEP supports and works with the renewable energy and energy efficiency industries and industry professionals. It has been offering its solar PV installer certification exam for highly experienced installers since 2003. The NABCEP also has an entry-level exam program for beginning installers who want to get jobs in the solar industry.

Wind Turbine Technician

What Does a Wind Turbine Technician Do?

A wind turbine technician—also called a windtech—inspects, maintains, tests, and repairs wind turbine equipment. Wind turbines, rising hundreds of feet into the air and arrayed in long rows in rural areas, outside cities and towns, and offshore in coastal regions, convert wind currents into affordable electricity. Neighborhood homes also sport smaller turbines in backyards to generate power and cut dependence on the electric power grid. According to the American Wind Energy Association, there are more than forty-eight thousand wind turbines operating in the United States. The positive outlook for wind turbine technician jobs matches the strong forecast for the wind power industry as a whole. In 2014 the US Department of Energy (DOE) updated its *Wind Vision Report*. The DOE predicts that by 2050 wind power could save consumers

$280 billion in energy costs and provide more than six hundred thousand jobs in manufacturing, installation, maintenance, and support services. Experts believe that as costs come down the industry could continue to see enormous growth in the years ahead. "Wind currently accounts for less than five percent of the total electricity generated in the US," notes technology writer John Timmer. "That stands in stark contrast with the total potential for wind power, which is more than 10 times our current electrical consumption."

As wind energy has become a reliable power source, the value of wind turbine technicians has risen. Wind energy companies depend on these technicians to diagnose problems and fix them before the giant turbines are forced to shut down and stop producing power. Typically, technicians climb the turbine's tower to inspect its exterior and working parts, particularly in the nacelle where electricity is produced. They may perform routine maintenance or react to problems detected by twenty-four-hour electronic monitors. When a problem is found, technicians must be ready to travel to the site of the turbine. Since wind farms are often located in remote areas, travel time may be considerable. Repairs may call for replacing a worn-out part or adjusting a component that is malfunctioning. There is pressure for technicians to find the problem and fix it quickly so that turbines are not idle for long. The most valued wind turbine technicians often have expert electrician skills to speed up the repair process.

An energy company loses money every hour that a turbine is offline on a windy day. "Turbine availability is an important metric, but never more so than when the wind is blowing," says Jason Allen, a manager at Duke Energy, in the online magazine *Wind Systems*. "It's bad to have a turbine come back online just in time for the wind to die down. It's even worse to have a technician performing routine work on a turbine when we could be producing electricity at peak capacity due to very windy conditions." Technicians may work on a troubleshooting team, traveling to the site of a malfunctioning turbine to find the source of the trouble. Many techs enjoy this part of the job, which calls for close analysis and reasoning, like industrial detective work. When a hunch proves correct and the turbine is repaired, the result is especially satisfying.

How Do You Become a Wind Turbine Technician?

Education

Most wind turbine technicians prepare to enter the field by taking a two-year associate's degree program at a technical school or community college. A background in mechanical work, such as experience as an auto mechanic or electrician, is helpful for prospective technicians. Trade school programs teach the basics of wind turbine technology with some information about engineering and applied sciences. Some schools have on-site wind turbines so students can get hands-on training. Candidates should seek teachers who are knowledgeable about the latest turbine technology and perhaps have worked in the industry.

Students at a trade school or community college focus on electrical wiring, hydraulic maintenance, braking systems, and inspection of blades and mechanical systems. They also study computers and programmable logic control systems. These systems monitor changes in wind speed and direction to realign the giant rotor blades for maximum performance. Overall, students get a thorough introduction to wind turbines, including how to install, inspect, troubleshoot, and repair their complex machinery. They also learn safety procedures and high-angle rescue techniques, plus receive training in first aid and CPR. With demand for technicians on the rise, some wind energy firms are hiring students enrolled in associate programs before they complete their studies.

Training and Certification

Wind energy companies invest $4 million to $6 million (not including installation) on each wind turbine, so they demand first-rate technicians for repairs and maintenance. Many companies offer on-the-job training programs for qualified entry-level wind turbine technicians. These yearlong programs typically focus on the particular style of turbines to be serviced. Turbine manufacturers may conduct their own training. Candidates may also get training through an internship program offered by an outside service contractor. A key feature of most basic training programs is learning how to assemble a wind turbine completely from its parts. This provides the kind of detailed knowledge about turbines that helps a technician troubleshoot problems with confidence.

A wind turbine technician checks a turbine for proper function. These technicians inspect, maintain, test, and repair wind turbine equipment. They also diagnose and fix problems as they arise.

Certification for wind turbine technicians is not mandatory, but it can be useful as proof of expertise and professional experience.

Skills and Personality

A wind turbine technician must be an excellent mechanic, able to work with a variety of tools and power equipment. He or she should have strong communication skills and be able to work well with a team. An entry-level technician must listen closely to supervisors and follow directions with care. He or she must also be able to learn quickly by observing the process of making repairs or checking for malfunctions. A technician benefits from having a strong sense of curiosity and a logical approach to problem solving. He or she must also have the ability to work independently and make rapid decisions in stressful situations. Wind farms tend to be isolated, and wind turbine technicians are often the first to respond when there is an accident or emergency. It is vital that they are able to diagnose the problem quickly and complete the necessary repairs so that the turbine is not idle for long. Mechanical work on turbines can call for long hours and detailed procedures, so the technician must have a solid work ethic.

On the Job

Employers

The US Bureau of Labor Statistics (BLS) says that about 24 percent of wind turbine technician jobs are with companies that generate or transmit electric power. About the same percentage of technician jobs are in utility system construction. Another 23 percent of windtech jobs are with original equipment manufacturers that design and assemble the turbines. These companies provide warranties for their turbines that extend from two to five years. They employ wind turbine technicians to do repairs and maintenance during the warranty period. In coming years the best jobs for wind turbine technicians are likely to be with energy companies that are building wind farms offshore, such as Providence, Rhode Island–based Deepwater Wind. These facilities should provide lucrative work for installers, troubleshooters, maintenance personnel, and supervisors.

Working Conditions

Wind turbine technicians perform their job outdoors in all weather conditions. They must climb ladders that reach 260 feet (79 m) into the air while carrying a variety of tools and wearing a harness to protect against falling. They must be comfortable working at great heights and with high-powered, often complex machinery. Technicians must squeeze into the nacelle to perform repairs on electrical equipment or rappel on ropes to clean or adjust turbine blades. These maneuvers require the technician to be physically fit in order to perform strenuous tasks and also have a certain amount of agility. "It takes a special breed of person to become a wind technician," says Fred Sellers in an interview on the website Windpower Engineering & Development. Sellers, a General Electric site manager for 305 turbines in Panther Creek, Texas, observes, "You have to be physically able to handle the strain that climbing the turbine puts on your body and you have to be smart enough to solve technical challenges on the equipment."

The job also involves a good deal of risk and calls for adherence to safe work practices. Wind turbine facilities can present many dangers, from toxic chemicals to hazardous machinery to electrical shocks. Every technician must abide by company safety guidelines without fail. Despite the challenging nature of the work, surveys suggest that a majority of wind turbine technicians find their job highly satisfying.

Earnings

According to the BLS, in 2015 the median annual wage for wind turbine technicians was $51,050. Wages for technicians at electric power companies averaged a bit more, at $54,760. The highest 10 percent of technicians earned more than $71,820, and the lowest 10 percent made a little more than half that, at $37,010. South Dakota, North Dakota, and Kansas were the states offering the highest annual mean wages for wind turbine technicians.

What Is the Future Outlook for Wind Turbine Technicians?

The BLS projects that employment for wind turbine technicians will grow by 108 percent through 2024, a rate that is far above the average for all occupations. The small size of this occupation means that the rapid growth will produce only about forty-eight hundred new jobs. Nonetheless, exciting technological developments in wind energy—including offshore installations, taller towers, larger blades, and even bladeless turbines—promise more opportunities in the industry. The number of turbines being installed should continue to increase, resulting in more jobs for technicians, particularly those willing to relocate to states focusing on wind energy.

Find Out More

American Wind Energy Association (AWEA)
1501 M St. NW, Suite 1000
Washington, DC 20005
website: www.awea.org

The AWEA is the premier national trade association for American wind energy. It promotes wind turbine technicians as America's fastest growing profession, needed to service the more than fifty thousand wind turbines in the country.

Ecotech Institute
website: www.ecotechinstitute.com

The Ecotech Institute is a college offering courses in renewable energy and management. On the Ecotech website, prospective wind turbine technicians can obtain a free e-book on starting a career in wind energy. The e-book contains a helpful section on the job requirements for a wind turbine technician.

Wind Energy Foundation
website: http://windenergyfoundation.org

The Wind Energy Foundation was started by senior executives in the wind industry in 2010 to offer research and education on wind energy and promote wind energy growth. Its website discusses the many careers available in wind energy, including wind turbine technician.

WindTurbineTechnicians.net
website: www.windturbinetechnicians.net

This website provides lots of valuable information about a career as a wind turbine technician, including training, schools, job types, job listings, and salaries.

Energy Consultant

What Does an Energy Consultant Do?

At a Glance:

Energy Consultant

Minimum Educational Requirements
Bachelor's degree, generally in some form of engineering

Personal Qualities
Self-confident; industrious; perceptive

Valuable Skills
Excellent communication skills, both speaking and writing; ability to work well with others; logical reasoning skills; ability to solve problems and design solutions

Working Conditions
At a computer in an office; travel to client facilities

Salary Range
About $41,000 to $97,000

Number of Jobs
As of 2014, in the United States there were 758,000 management analysts and consultants—a group that includes energy consultants

Future Job Outlook
Growth rate of 14 percent through 2024

An energy consultant works with businesses and residential customers to help them reduce energy costs. The consultant helps identify the best and most efficient use of energy sources for the client's particular situation. This generally includes the use of natural gas, electricity, and other sources for producing energy. With conservation and sustainability so important in today's business world, many energy consultants choose to focus entirely on green solutions—clean, renewable sources of energy. Some consultants work with only one source, such as solar energy or wind power. A background in engineering or science can help them stay current with the latest green energy technology. A savvy energy consultant may also function as a broker, negotiating with energy companies to get the best deal for his or her client. In addition, a consultant might offer to track utility bills for a company or household to ensure that the client is not being overcharged for power. With hard work and imagination, an energy consultant can impact a company's bottom line by saving significant amounts in energy costs while also promoting responsible policies toward the environment.

The primary job of an energy consultant is to inform the client about the various options for energy use. The consultant then identifies the options that he or she believes will provide the necessary volume and type of energy at the lowest cost. Once the client makes a decision, the consultant will set about securing that energy option at the best possible price.

Few companies have their own energy consultant on the payroll. Hiring a consultant enables a company to enlist the services of one or more trained professionals who can diagnose problems and needs from the outside. Generally, an energy consultant begins by reviewing a company's previous energy bills. This audit helps the consultant understand how the company uses energy. It can also reveal mischarged fees or a pattern of billing mistakes by a utility company. Here a consultant's expertise on local energy rate schedules and utility company tariffs can be very helpful. (A tariff is a set of rules that defines the relationship between a utility and its customers.) Evidence of overcharging represents money that the consultant can have refunded or applied to future bills.

Next, the energy consultant spends time with the client and examines facilities closely to understand how the business uses energy and to assess the company's needs. Here the consultant can benefit from training as an engineer and learning to read an electrical diagram (for wiring setups) or psychometric chart (for heat load and cooling load related to air-conditioning problems). The consultant uses this assessment to create a technical report for the client (often with the assistance of other engineers) and to draw up a plan on how to reduce the company's overall energy use or increase its efficiency. For example, the consultant might find areas to save money, such as improving building insulation, replacing a heat pump, or switching to more energy-efficient LED lighting or newer-model air-conditioning units. He or she might also recommend even more high-tech solutions, such as setting up a smart system of meters, thermostats, and sensors programmed to save energy. Such computerized systems are part of the Internet of Things, in which sensors enable machines and appliances to communicate with each other and power up or down automatically depending on times of highest usage. The system also provides the energy consultant with vast amounts of data to identify precisely where energy is being wasted. Ken Sinclair, a long-time energy consultant, sees so-called smart buildings as one of the most important innovations in conserving energy. In an interview on the website Building Efficiency Initiative.org, Sinclair observes, "We now have the secret sauce to make large buildings or groups of smaller buildings interact with the smart grid. The energy Internet can rapidly interact with the supply grid. For the first time, supply and demand can talk and cooperate. We can achieve action and reaction in real time without manual intervention."

Riptide, a California-based energy consulting firm, produced great savings in energy costs for US drugstore chain Walgreens. The smart-building system that Riptide provided for thousands of Walgreens stores nationwide—at a total cost of $20 million saved Walgreens $14 million in its first year alone. Riptide also helped one Walgreens outlet in Chicago achieve net-zero energy, meaning it produced more energy than it used from the power grid. This was achieved by incorporating solar panels, wind turbines, and LED lighting in a comprehensive energy package. When a company decides to take this step, an energy consultant can oversee the implementation of the new technology.

Employing green solutions like these, as well as advising firms to replace gas-guzzling company cars with hybrids and electric models, has become a major selling point for many energy consultants. They also inform companies about government grants and loan programs that can provide assistance in switching to more energy-efficient operations. An energy consultant can also tout the public relations value of embracing environmentally friendly options. Some energy consulting firms present seminars to educate local companies about energy use and green technologies—and in the process advertise their own services.

Finally, an energy consultant can act as a broker—an intermediary between buyer and seller, like a stockbroker. The consultant can arrange a service contract between a homeowner and a local utility provider. For businesses both large and small, the consultant can negotiate contracts with utilities to get favorable terms. In areas where local utilities are unregulated, businesses have a choice of which provider to use. The broker can use this competition to obtain lower electricity rates for his or her client. Utility data is complex and calls for great skill and expertise to convert it to decision-ready information. A successful energy consultant also stays abreast of world energy markets, local and federal tax laws, and market opportunities. A business client is often more than willing to pay to have a consultant assume the responsibility of finding the best deals for energy.

How Do You Become an Energy Consultant?

Education

Most, but not all, energy consultants have a background in engineering. Students who seek a career in energy consulting should consider taking undergraduate courses in engineering, environmental science, mathematics, physics, and business management.

Although universities do not have bachelor's programs specifically for energy consulting, some schools offer specialized programs that teach many useful skills for this occupation. These include building-inspection techniques such as how to do a blower-door test to measure the airtightness of a building and its ductwork and how to perform thermographic inspections, which test for the release of heat from parts, materials, or systems. Students might also learn basic information about construction and insulation. Some schools offer a master's degree in sustainability and energy management. These programs include such topics as the principles of energy conservation, calibrating instruments, inspecting for energy loss, and preparing analyses and reports.

In general, employers would like energy consultants to have at least a bachelor's degree. Candidates commonly work for two or three years under the supervision of a seasoned energy consultant to get real-world experience in the field. Trainees who have more academic credentials may require fewer hours of supervised training.

Certification

Energy consultants typically do not have to be certified in the United States or Canada. However, certification can enhance their status as professionals and assure clients of their managerial, financial, and technical expertise with regard to energy issues. Some states offer certification through a public utilities commission. The Leadership in Energy and Environmental Design certification programs are internationally recognized and show that the consultant is qualified to design and carry out green energy projects. These programs are offered through certain schools that are authorized by the US Green Building Council.

Skills and Personality

Communication skills are paramount for an energy consultant, particularly the ability to explain complex issues in plain language. The website of the Independent Energy Consultants advises employers, "Ideally look for someone who can identify problems in the boiler room and explain solutions in the boardroom." A successful energy consultant is always attentive to detail and strives to keep up with the latest tax laws, subsidies, and tech innovations. He or she must be a problem solver able to weigh the pros and cons of a potential solution. A consultant should have excellent math skills and enough knowledge in building science and engineering to perform detailed site reviews alone or with a team. Computer skills and the ability to frame proposals in a digital format are also helpful.

With regard to personality and character, energy consultants must be dependable, cooperative, and adaptable to the different workplaces they find. Integrity is essential, as clients must be assured of the consultant's honesty and ethical approach. The ability to handle stress and maintain focus throughout a long process is also important.

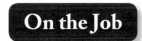

On the Job

Employers

An energy consultant may work for a large national or international company that employs several hundred consultants in various areas.

He or she might also choose to work at a small firm or set up as an independent energy consultant. Some companies specialize in consulting on alternative energy solutions or even on one type of green energy, such as wind or solar. An independent energy consultant may focus on residential jobs and can even work from home and market his or her services online or door to door. A common career path for an ambitious energy consultant is to train for two or three years with a large company and then leave to start a consulting business with a group of like-minded associates.

Working Conditions

Energy consultants split their workday between an ordinary office environment and visits to client facilities. A consultant at a large firm may make frequent trips around the country or to international destinations. Some consultants for multinational firms end up relocating overseas. When assessing buildings or factory sites, the consultant is often on his or her feet for hours at a time and may have to squeeze into tight places to make an inspection.

Earnings

According to the website PayScale, the median annual wage for energy consultants in the United States is $62,441. The salary range is $41,047 to $97,909. At the upper levels of the occupation, bonuses can total more than $15,000 a year and profit sharing more than $9,500.

What Is the Future Outlook for Energy Consultants?

The US Bureau of Labor Statistics does not include information specifically about energy consultants. However, it projects that demand for consulting services in general should show healthy growth as businesses seek to improve their efficiency and control costs. Employment numbers for management analysts, a category that includes energy consultants, were 758,000 in 2014 and are projected to climb to 861,400 in 2024, a growth rate of 14 percent.

Find Out More

Association of Energy Engineers (AEE)
3168 Mercer University Dr.
Atlanta, GA 30341
website: www.aeecenter.org

The AEE promotes the scientific and educational interests of those in the energy industry. It offers a certified energy auditor program that is beneficial for energy consultants.

Independent Energy Consultants (IEC)
website: www.naturalgas-electric.com

The IEC is an independent consulting company that is licensed to develop municipal programs for electricity and natural gas. Although the IEC is not focused on green energy, its website contains helpful information about what an energy consultant does.

Summit Energy
website: www.summitenergy.com

Summit Energy has a worldwide team of more than 850 energy consultants dealing with creative energy solutions and sustainability for businesses. Its website features case studies that demonstrate how Summit professionals have helped large companies realize significant energy savings.

US Green Building Council (USGBC)
website: www.usgbc.org

The USGBC offers the Leadership in Energy and Environmental Design (LEED) program, which certifies the knowledge, experience, and expertise of building consultants with regard to being environmentally sound and efficient in the use of resources. LEED certification indicates that an energy consultant is expert at employing green solutions.

Air Quality Forecaster

What Does an Air Quality Forecaster Do?

An air quality forecaster predicts the level of pollutants in the air in a given city, state, or region. Each year, air pollution causes an estimated 3.7 million premature deaths worldwide, and it also ravages crops capable of feeding millions. Air pollution remains one of the largest environmental risks to health and food security. The public has come to expect daily weather forecasts to include information on air quality. In fact, today's weather forecasts generally include predictions about temperature, wind speed, ultraviolet levels (for risk of sun exposure), pollen counts, and a report on ozone levels and particulate matter in the air. An air quality forecaster works alongside other meteorologists to study the human impact on the atmosphere and predict how air pollution levels will vary from day to day.

Information about air quality helps people take precautions to protect their health, such as avoiding outdoor work

---

At a Glance:
Air Quality Forecaster

Minimum Educational Requirements
Bachelor's degree

Personal Qualities
Hardworking; inquisitive; able to collaborate

Valuable Skills
Communication and computer skills; mathematical ability

Working Conditions
Indoors and some outdoors

Salary Range
About $71,000 to $100,000

Number of Jobs
As of 2014 there were about 11,800 atmospheric scientists and meteorologists, including air quality forecasters

Future Job Outlook
Growth rate of 9 percent through 2024

---

or activity when pollution levels are forecast to be high. Many areas in and around cities have problems with ground-level ozone—so-called bad ozone—that is created when human-made emissions of certain organic compounds and nitrogen oxides interact in the presence of direct sunlight. Ground-level ozone can irritate a person's respiratory system, reduce lung function, and trigger asthma attacks. With prolonged exposure, it can cause permanent lung damage. To help people stay informed about ozone dangers, the US Environmental Protection Agency (EPA) created the Air Quality Index (AQI). The AQI is a color-coded scale (green-yellow orange-red-purple) that shows the level of ozone and other pollutants in the air, usually for an eight-hour period. Code Green indicates good air conditions, Code Orange is bad for sensitive groups, and Code Purple is considered very unhealthy overall. An air quality forecaster uses the AQI to tell the public what to expect each day with regard to ozone pollution.

Before he or she can predict air quality, a forecaster must work with meteorologists to determine the current weather forecast, including the approach of fronts and changes in temperature and cloud cover. The air quality forecaster uses data from the past, present, and future—conditions for the previous day or days, real-time data on current conditions, and computer models that predict future conditions. He or she also consults satellite data and images and daily weather maps. The technique is based on persistence forecasting, in which each day's air quality forecast proceeds from what happened the day before. Gradual changes are the rule until some disruptive event occurs, such as a cold front or a wildfire. Pollutants can also build up gradually over several days of similar weather, such as sunny and hot conditions, until safe Code Yellow readings become unhealthy at Code Red.

New technology is also changing the field. The planned launch of new satellites over the next several years promises to make air quality forecasting even more reliable. So-called geostationary satellites will orbit Earth at a height of 22,000 miles (35,406 km) above the equator. Such satellites, normally employed for telecommunications and weather imaging, can provide precise hourly measures of smoke, dust, and other pollutants in the atmosphere at different altitudes. Combined with readouts collected from satellites in lower orbits, the new data will enable air quality forecasters to make more precise predictions and create even more useful computer models. They can also use geographic information system (GIS) data to make their forecasts. GIS software helps the forecaster capture, analyze, display, and share all types of geographic data in the form of maps, globes, tables, and charts. This enables the forecaster to spot patterns and trends in air quality that would otherwise be hidden. Data from these technologies can be supported with field studies and other forms of research.

Like a meteorologist whose weather forecasts can save lives, an air quality forecaster feels a responsibility to alert the public about unhealthy conditions. "Just as our television meteorologists sometimes miss whether it will be cloudy or sunny in our area, sometimes we will miss the actual PM2.5 (measure of fine particulate matter) and ozone category or color code for the day," writes a meteorology blogger for Nashville.gov. "If there is any question as to how a day will be forecast, we will make every effort to err on the side of over predicting the expected maximum concentration as the intent of this forecasting process is to protect the health of the citizens of Middle Tennessee."

An air quality forecaster performs many tasks related to the overall goal of gauging air quality. Some work for government agencies or private companies that have specific needs for their expertise. For example, an air quality forecaster might study yields of certain crops in relation to ozone levels. He or she might provide expert advice on developing regulations for clean air or help determine why certain demographic groups are more vulnerable to high ozone levels and airborne pollutants. A forecaster might work alongside engineers and technicians to ensure that emission-control programs are implemented properly for a private manufacturing business. Commercial and private aviation agencies hire air quality forecasters to advise them on appropriate safety precautions in hazy skies caused by pollution. At all times and in whatever position, a forecaster must read widely about current research in meteorology and related fields.

How Do You Become an Air Quality Forecaster?

Education

At present, air quality forecasting is too specialized a field to have its own degree program in colleges. Most students who want to pursue air quality forecasting as a career begin by studying one of the earth sciences, such as geography or geology, while also gaining a background in physics, chemistry, and mathematics. Students should then focus on meteorology or atmospheric science. A bachelor's degree in atmospheric science is sufficient for most jobs related to air quality forecasting. Students should also take courses in computer programming because they will have to write and edit the kinds of software programs used to create forecasts. Today's technology calls for a class in remote sensing of the environment, such as by satellite or radar.

For a more advanced position in research, such as working for a policy-making agency, a master's degree is very helpful although not essential. To enter a master's program in meteorology, the applicant might earn an undergraduate degree in math or in a scientific field like chemistry, biology, or physics. A doctorate is probably necessary for more specialized research and teaching positions at a college or university.

Certification and Training

Air quality forecasters can become certified through the American Meteorological Society's Certified Consulting Meteorologist (CCM) Program. According to the society's website, "The principal purpose of the program is to enable users of meteorological services to select consultants with greater confidence in the quality and reliability of the products and services they will receive. CCMs must demonstrate exemplary qualities of character and devotion to high professional standards."

Training requirements for air quality forecasters vary according to their place of employment. The National Weather Service requires meteorologists and atmospheric scientists to receive two hundred hours of on-the-job training in each of their first two years of working at the service.

Skills and Personality

To prepare their forecasts, air quality forecasters must be able to spend long hours analyzing computer models and different data sources. With forecasts usually varying only slightly from day to day, the forecaster must be able to discern subtle patterns in the data to see emerging trends. Mathematical skills, including the use of calculus, statistics, and other advanced forms, are essential for probing the interrelationship of atmospheric properties, weather phenomena, and pollutants. The forecaster must also have excellent critical-thinking skills and the ability to solve problems. Skill in writing and speaking clearly enables the forecaster to communicate more effectively with employers, peers and coworkers, and the public. Air quality forecasters who advance to higher positions must demonstrate leadership abilities in directing projects in the field and managing employees and assistants. In general, a forecaster should possess patience, curiosity, and enthusiasm for work that can affect people's health on a daily basis.

On the Job

Employers

An experienced air quality forecaster can work in many different areas. One common job is with a meteorological organization, whether state, national, or international. These forecasters gather meteorological data and use it to create computer models that help them predict air quality. Other jobs for air quality forecasters are found in US government agencies such as the EPA, the National Oceanic and Atmospheric Administration, and the National Park Service. Forecasters may also work in education and meteorological research. A large corporation may hire an air quality forecaster to determine how its business affects local air quality. Health groups may hire a forecaster to determine how air pollution affects people with specific medical conditions. Agricultural organizations might enlist air quality forecasters to study the effects of specific pollutants on certain crops. With the growing emphasis on the environment worldwide, air quality forecasters promise to be in great demand for the foreseeable future.

Working Conditions

Air quality forecasters generally work indoors, although they may do occasional fieldwork. At weather monitoring facilities or laboratories, they may spend hours in front of the computer screen analyzing data and converting statistical models to graphics. Forecasters may also spend considerable time discussing trends and conditions with other meteorologists and atmospheric scientists.

Earnings

As a discipline closely related to meteorology, air quality forecasting has the same basic salary structure. According to the US Bureau of Labor Statistics (BLS), the median annual wage for 2015 was $89,820. Federal government jobs paid the highest of any sector with a median salary of $99,920. Consultant jobs paid only slightly less, at $87,370. Air quality forecasters working in education make a little more than $71,000 a year.

What Is the Future Outlook for Air Quality Forecasters?

The BLS projects a 9 percent increase in job demand for air quality forecasters through 2024. This rising demand is expected to hold for all areas that hire forecasters, including the public and private sectors, research groups, and academic institutions. Job growth for air quality forecasters should be especially strong among energy companies, particularly those in renewable energy, which increasingly need specialized data about weather, climate, and air pollution.

Find Out More

Agricultural Air Quality Task Force
website: www.nrcs.usda.gov

The Agricultural Air Quality Task Force, part of the US Department of Agriculture, leads the study of air quality issues nationwide. The agency's website includes information about its mission and research projects.

American Geosciences Institute (AGI)
4220 King St.
Alexandria, VA 22302
website: www.americangeosciences.org

The AGI provides information services to geoscientists, including meteorologists, and plays an important role in promoting education in geoscience. It also tries to further public awareness of the crucial role that geoscientists play in society's use of resources and pursuit of a healthy environment.

National Oceanic and Atmospheric Administration (NOAA)
1401 Constitution Ave. NW, Room 5128
Washington, DC 20230
website: www.noaa.gov

NOAA works to keep citizens informed about changes in the environment, from the upper atmosphere to the ocean floor. It provides daily weather forecasts, severe storm warnings, and air quality forecasts through the National Weather Service.

World Meteorological Organization (WMO)
website: http://public.wmo.int/en

The WMO, a division of the World Health Organization, helps set the policy on environmental issues for the United Nations. It funds meteorological research that also touches on pollutants and overall air quality.

Petroleum Engineer

What Does a Petroleum Engineer Do?

A petroleum engineer designs and develops the most efficient ways to drill for and extract oil and/or natural gas from a well site. Petroleum engineers also monitor drilling operations and deal with problems in oil production. They perform tests to evaluate how much oil and gas are being produced and try to stimulate production at wells that are not performing as expected. Petroleum engineers are always looking to develop more efficient tools and technologies for extracting oil and gas. They are also constantly studying the geology of potential well sites to determine where to begin future drilling projects.

Although the public and private sectors are intent on developing renewable sources of clean energy, the fossil fuel industry is not going away. In July 2015 analysts at Rystad Energy, an independent oil consulting service, estimated that the United States may possess as much as 264 billion barrels of oil underground, compared to the 212 billion barrels in Saudi Arabia. Overall, the Rystad analysts project that worldwide oil

At a Glance:
Petroleum Engineer

Minimum Educational Requirements
Bachelor's degree

Personal Qualities
Curiosity; patience; resourcefulness

Valuable Skills
Reasoning and problem-solving skills; computer skills

Working Conditions
Indoors in offices and labs; outdoors at well sites

Salary Range
About $74,880 to $187,200

Number of Jobs
As of 2014 about 35,100

Future Job Outlook
Growth rate of 10 percent through 2024

reserves may amount to more than 2 trillion barrels, enough to meet the world's demand for seventy years. This enormous increase in estimated oil reserves is due to the work of petroleum engineers and the technological breakthroughs they have made in drilling and extraction methods. Despite the growth of green energy and the rollercoaster ride of oil prices, the oil industry promises to offer plenty of good job opportunities for the foreseeable future.

Petroleum engineers seek deposits of oil and gas, called reservoirs, which are found in rock formations deep underground. Petroleum engineers in the field can specialize in different areas of the extraction process. When oil is discovered, reservoir engineers estimate the amount of oil that can be recovered from the reservoir. They also work with geoscientists and other experts to survey the surrounding rock formation and determine the extraction methods that will maximize production. Subsurface engineers—also called completions engineers—select the equipment that best suits the subsurface environment of the well. In essence, they make sure the well is ready for production. They work closely with drilling engineers, who decide on a drilling method, design the appropriate drilling equipment, and set the drilling plan in motion. The drilling engineer must consider many factors, including cost, safety, efficiency, and environmental impact. Once drilling is completed and the plan is operating, the production engineer monitors the well's production and troubleshoots any problems that arise.

In an interview on the website Energy4Me, Mollie, a veteran petroleum engineer, emphasizes that the job is never static. "My job is always changing," she notes.

> Working in operations I have many roles to fill and I have to make decisions that impact our business. If tools/equipment break in the field, you have to use the resources available to you to fix it and you might not have a backup piece of equipment. You become very good, very quickly at all sorts of things: electrical wiring, computer repair, diesel engine maintenance just to name a few.

New technologies are revolutionizing the oil and gas business and are providing more opportunities for petroleum engineers, particularly in the United States. An extraction technology called hydraulic fracturing, or fracking, taps into previously inaccessible oil and gas deposits locked in rock formations deep underground. The fracking boom doubled the number of natural gas wells in the United States between 2000 and 2010. About thirteen thousand new wells are drilled every year in places like the Marcellus shale formation in Pennsylvania and the Bakken shale formation in North Dakota. Despite plummeting prices for oil and natural gas in recent years, petroleum engineers who can oversee this process and get the highest possible production from fracking sites promise to be in great demand in the future.

A petroleum engineer can spend as much time in front of a computer screen as at a well site. He or she might create a computer simulation to forecast the amount and flow of oil and natural gas in a well. Since only a small fraction of oil and gas in a reservoir will flow out naturally after drilling, a petroleum engineer must design various ways to increase recovery. This can mean forcing the product out of the reservoir by injecting it with water, chemicals, gases, or steam. Computer simulations can help the petroleum engineer decide which method will likely work best. He or she might also employ computer-controlled drilling to help avoid problems with hole cleaning, stuck pipe, pressure changes, and torque and drag in the drilling process. Computers are programmed to control the speed, force, and depth of the drill for better safety and efficiency, and the engineer monitors the data that computer sensors collect during the drilling process. Although computers play an important role, the petroleum engineer must constantly make decisions about how to proceed in developing a well and maximizing production.

How Do You Become a Petroleum Engineer?

Education
In high school, taking courses in math and science is the best preparation for a career as a petroleum engineer. Math courses should include algebra, trigonometry, and calculus, and science classes such as biology, chemistry, and physics are extremely helpful. An entry-level job as a petroleum engineer generally requires, at minimum, a bachelor's

degree in some form of engineering. Many colleges and universities offer petroleum engineering programs that are certified by the Accreditation Board of Engineering and Technology. A bachelor's degree program for petroleum engineers includes not only classes but also extensive lab work and field studies in related disciplines, such as geology, thermodynamics, and mechanical engineering. Many institutions feature cooperative programs, giving students a chance to do fieldwork in the industry while working toward a degree.

Some schools also offer a five-year program for a bachelor's or master's degree in petroleum engineering. Certain energy companies may favor candidates with an advanced degree. A graduate degree also gives a petroleum engineer the option of teaching or doing well-paid research.

Certification and Training

Certification, although not required for entry-level jobs in petroleum engineering, can enhance job opportunities and attract larger wages. The Society of Petroleum Engineers (SPE) offers a certification exam for its members as well as an online review course to prepare for the exam. Members must also have an undergraduate degree in petroleum engineering or a related engineering degree and at least four years of experience and training. Certification by the SPE provides the petroleum engineer with a credential that is recognized internationally. Petroleum engineers can also obtain a professional engineering license, which is generally recognized in all states.

Skills and Personality

Whether on a drill site or at a computer in an office, a petroleum engineer must excel at identifying and solving problems. Drilling operation costs can soar if delays occur or equipment malfunctions. Engineers must be able to address problems rapidly and come up with imaginative solutions. They must also be able to analyze projects in the planning stages and spot potential flaws or difficulties that could end up costing their company huge amounts of money. Since each new drilling site presents its own particular set of problems, petroleum engineers must be creative in finding the best possible methods for extracting oil and gas. The ability to work and communicate with a crew of professionals in stressful situations is also crucial to an engineer's success. Petroleum engineers must know what questions to ask and how to maximize the efficiency of his or her crew. They tend to be calm under pressure, attentive to details, confident, authoritative, inquisitive, and resourceful.

On the Job

Employers

Due to the continuing importance of fossil fuels to the world economy, petroleum engineers have a wide range of employment opportunities. An engineer can work for a small drilling company—a so-called wildcat firm—whose activity is restricted to one state or area. He or she can join a large energy company that has production fields all over the world and is always seeking new strikes. Many petroleum engineers spend years working overseas, either traveling frequently or relocating to another country. Some experienced engineers find lucrative opportunities with oil field equipment firms or oil industry analysts. Those with advanced degrees can choose to work in the public or private sector doing research or can teach at a college or university.

Working Conditions

Petroleum engineering is full-time work—in fact, it often calls for more than forty hours per week. An engineer must be prepared to travel to well sites and respond to emergencies at a moment's notice. Sites can be in remote areas that are difficult to reach or offshore in the ocean. At a well site, engineers often work in rotation shifts of eighty-four hours on and eighty-four hours off. Most engineers split time between office and drilling sites, with perhaps some laboratory work interspersed as well.

Earnings

According to the US Bureau of Labor Statistics (BLS), petroleum engineers consistently rank among the highest paid engineers of any discipline. In May 2015, the BLS listed the median annual wage for all petroleum engineers at $129,990. The upper 10 percent of the profession had annual wages of more than $187,200. Petroleum engineers in engineering services had the highest median annual wage at $155,940, with those in company management just behind at $152,450.

Opportunities for Advancement

Energy companies usually direct experienced petroleum engineers to train or supervise entry-level engineers. Once they have encountered a variety of work situations, young engineers can advance to solve problems, make well site decisions, and create equipment designs on their own. Ultimately, a knowledgeable petroleum engineer can lead her or his own team of technicians and engineers or work in a management position. Some experienced engineers join oil field equipment companies to develop products, supervise installation, or manage sales.

What Is the Future Outlook for Petroleum Engineers?

Tumbling oil prices in recent years have led to huge job losses at energy companies. This in turn has caused students to steer away from petroleum engineering and related majors, leading some experts to make pessimistic forecasts about the industry. Tobias Read, chief executive officer of the staffing agency Swift Worldwide Resources, told CNBC, "It's going to be a real problem. I think we will find there's going to be a substantial shortage of [petroleum engineering] talent coming into the market." But this development could also present opportunities.

The BLS sees employment for petroleum engineers growing by 10 percent through 2024. This is faster growth than the average for all job categories. Despite recent weakness in prices for oil and natural gas, more petroleum engineers will likely be needed to replace those who are retiring and to manage the complex technology of new well sites.

Find Out More

American Institute of Mining, Metallurgical, and Petroleum Engineers (AIME)
website: www.aimehq.org

AIME was one of the first engineering societies founded in the United States. It represents more than 150,000 engineering professionals worldwide, including petroleum engineers.

National Society of Professional Engineers (NSPE)
1420 King St.
Alexandria, VA 22314
website: www.nspe.org

The NSPE was established in 1934 to provide licensed engineers with a group to address nontechnical professional concerns of all kinds. Its website includes job listings for professional engineers in various fields.

Society of Petroleum Engineers (SPE)
222 Palisades Creek Dr.
Richardson, TX 75080
website: www.spe.org

The SPE is a nonprofit organization that is dedicated to collecting and sharing technical knowledge concerning oil and gas exploration, development, and production. It also provides opportunities for oil and gas professionals to increase their technical competence in the field.

Fuel Cell Engineer

What Does a Fuel Cell Engineer Do?

One of the most promising sources of clean energy today is fuel cell technology. A fuel cell is a device that makes use of the chemical reaction between a fuel, usually hydrogen, and an oxidant, like oxygen, to generate electricity. In other words, a fuel cell does not burn fuel; instead, it converts chemical energy to electric power. Unlike fossil fuels, most fuel cells do not pollute. They produce energy while emitting only heat and water or water vapor. Fuel cell engineers mainly design and test new technologies that make fuel cells more reliable, efficient, and functional. This occupation calls for first-rate science and math skills to support cutting-edge research into fuel cells and help satisfy the world's energy needs in the future. As the website Inside Jobs puts it, "As a Fuel Cell Engineer, you spend your days crashing hydrogen and oxygen together in such a way that it produces enough energy to power a car."

Fuel cell engineers have discovered many more applications for the technology than simply propelling cars and vans. In the field of transportation alone, fuel cells are capable of powering a range of smaller vehicles, such as light manned aircraft, ferries, boats, trams, forklifts, scooters, and unmanned aerial vehicles, or drones. They are especially useful as power sources in remote areas where other power sources are hard to access or too expensive. These might include a polar weather station, an isolated military facility, or a spacecraft. Portable fuel cells can be built into other equipment, such as a soldier's pack, flashlight, laptop, or electronic game. For portable use, fuel cells have the advantage of operating off the grid, running longer than batteries, and recharging rapidly. For stationary use, fuel cells can make up so-called uninterruptible power systems that provide guaranteed electricity should grid connection be disrupted. This is important for telecommunication base stations and data centers. In addition to applying these uses, a fuel cell engineer is always searching for new applications and breakthroughs for the technology.

Another goal of the fuel cell engineer's research is to make fuel cells a completely nonpolluting source of power. This calls for the clean production of hydrogen, the light gas on which most fuel cells operate. An important challenge facing the fuel cell engineer today is to improve the cost structure and efficiency of producing hydrogen cleanly, using renewable means rather than fossil fuels. One method, called electrolysis, uses an electric current to split water into its component elements of hydrogen and oxygen. If the electric current is produced by solar energy or wind power, the entire process remains carbon-free and better for the environment.

In 2016 the Swedish home furnishings company Ikea installed biogas-powered fuel cell systems at several of its stores in California. The fuel cell system at Ikea's Costa Mesa store reduces carbon emissions by the equivalent of 1,315 tons (1,193 t) each year. For these systems, Ikea contracted with Bloom Energy, a California-based company that employs experts in solid oxide fuel cell technology. Some fuel cell designs, however, still release a small amount of the gas carbon dioxide. Fuel cell engineers hope to find methods of capturing this extra carbon dioxide before it is emitted into the atmosphere.

Testing is a major part of what fuel cell engineers do. Each fuel cell device consists of parts that are carefully designed to create the chemical reaction between hydrogen and oxygen. The engineer constantly tries to improve each component in the fuel cell assembly, which means exhaustive testing of each part. For example, the type of fuel cell mainly used for vehicles—called a polymer electrolyte membrane fuel cell—consists of precisely calibrated components. One of these components is a specially treated membrane that looks like plastic wrap and forms a gateway allowing in positively charged ions and blocking electrons. Through the research efforts of fuel cell engineers and materials scientists, this specially treated membrane has become incredibly thin—sometimes less than 20 microns—making it even more sensitive and thus more efficient.

In a typical day, a fuel cell engineer might conduct tests of fuel cell systems and subsystems and analyze test data using statistical software. Component tests are done at state-of-the-art test stations featuring the most sophisticated diagnostic equipment available. He or she might create prototypes of fuel cell assemblies or individual parts. Experiments might be designed to optimize a fuel cell's start-up protocol or improve its tolerance of contaminants in the air. Failed tests require concentrated analyses of what went wrong. Throughout the testing process, fuel cell engineers are constantly in touch with other departments, such as manufacturing or maintenance, to assure quality control going forward.

A fuel cell engineer must also write technical reports about testing and detailed proposals for new projects. To keep up with the latest advances in fuel cell technology, he or she must pore through current journals, make time for conferences related to the field, and discuss innovations with colleagues. Overall, fuel cell engineering is an exciting, fast-paced occupation that combines high-tech expertise with a passion for environmentalism.

How Do You Become a Fuel Cell Engineer?

Education

Admission to an undergraduate engineering school calls for a strong background both in mathematics, including algebra, geometry, trigonometry, and calculus; and in science, including biology, chemistry, and physics. The US Department of Energy (DOE) sponsors the National

Energy Education Development project to provide high school teachers and students with educational materials on fuel cell technology.

Almost all entry-level jobs for fuel cell engineers require a bachelor's degree in chemical engineering, mechanical engineering, electrical engineering, or materials science. Undergraduate degree programs in engineering are usually set for four years, but a fifth year may be required for many students. The first two years of a standard four-year college curriculum feature mathematics, basic sciences, social sciences, humanities, and introductory classes in engineering. The last two years are concentrated on engineering courses, with most focused on fuel cell engineering and related disciplines. Some students acquire a general engineering degree and then specialize in fuel cell technology in graduate school or on the job. To ascend to a faculty position or a career in research in fuel cell engineering, a candidate must have graduate training.

Training

Out of college, fuel cell engineers usually begin working under experienced engineers. Some large companies offer formal training in the form of classroom studies or seminars. As they gain work experience, fuel cell engineers are assigned independent projects involving design issues and problem solving. Some engineers are trained to specialize in one aspect of the technology or to oversee a team of other engineers and scientists.

Skills and Personality

The quest to make fuel cells more reliable and efficient requires fuel cell engineers to excel at systems analysis, or determining how changes in conditions or environment affect system operation. An engineer must have strong critical-thinking skills, with the ability to use logic and reasoning to identify the best solutions to problems. He or she must be able to conduct detailed inspections and tests to evaluate performance of fuel cells for quality control. The ability to troubleshoot in order to find the causes of operating errors and deal with them decisively is also vital. Mechanical skills with tools and equipment are often helpful, as is expertise in statistical software and lab work. Fuel cell engineers who rise to become team leaders should be able to direct, coordinate, and motivate personnel to achieve specific goals.

A fuel cell engineer must be creative and persistent, with an eye to discovering new solutions to difficult problems. The person should be curious about every aspect of a fuel cell development project and an active listener with other workers. He or she must be analytical and detail oriented. The fuel cell engineer must work easily with a team and be able to communicate with experts and specialists from fields other than engineering.

On the Job

Employers

Fuel cell technology is one of the ultimate energy pursuits of modern science. Fuel cell engineers are constantly working to develop fuel cells that can compete with fossil fuels and green technologies in the areas of energy production, delivery, and storage. This quest provides employment opportunities for engineers not only in private companies but also with the federal government and academic institutions. A fuel cell engineer might work for one of the large automakers that is developing fuel cell technology to power a fleet of electric or hybrid automobiles. For example, a recent General Motors job posting called for a "Fuel Cell Test Systems Engineer to specify, develop, qualify, implement, and continuously improve test [standards] and measurement systems used in hydrogen fuel cell materials and systems research and development activities." Private tech firms focused on fuel cell development are always looking for engineering talent, whether veterans of the industry or promising newcomers. The DOE also has its own fuel cell research unit with opportunities for engineers. In March 2015 the DOE announced a $35 million program to advance fuel cell and hydrogen-based technologies. Research units in colleges and universities also are excellent job sources for experienced fuel cell engineers.

Working Conditions

Fuel cell engineers generally work a forty-hour week, although project deadlines may occasionally require overtime hours. The work environment typically is indoors in office settings, laboratories, and industrial plants.

Earnings

According to Recruiter.com, annual wages for fuel cell engineers range from $64,000 to $96,000, depending on experience and academic background. The median wage is $82,180. Jobs in testing and statistical analysis tend to be at the lower end of the range, and research and development positions cluster at the higher end.

What Is the Future Outlook for Fuel Cell Engineers?

Although the job growth outlook for fuel cell engineers is below average at 3 to 6 percent, the demand may well be more favorable by 2026. Increased emphasis on clean energy solutions should deliver continued growth for hybrid and hydrogen fuel cell automobiles. As fuel cells become more reliable and cost-effective, engineers should be needed to design new uses for them. According to the DOE, global markets for fuel cell technology are likely to see huge expansion in the coming decade. Businesses that develop, manufacture, operate, and repair these systems will offer lucrative job opportunities for fuel cell engineers. Becoming a fuel cell engineer enables an individual to work for a cleaner environment and meet the challenge of finding practical solutions to the world's energy needs.

Find Out More

American Society for Engineering Education (ASEE)
1818 N St. NW, Suite 600
Washington, DC 20036
website: www.asee.org

The ASEE is a nonprofit organization of individuals and institutions committed to promoting education in engineering and engineering technology. Its more than twelve thousand members come from all disciplines of engineering, including fuel cell technology.

American Society of Mechanical Engineers (ASME)
Two Park Ave.
New York, NY 10016-5990
website: www.asme.org

The ASME is a nonprofit organization that promotes collaboration and knowledge sharing among all engineering disciplines. It is the world's leading developer of codes and standards for mechanical engineering.

Fuel Cell & Hydrogen Energy Association (FCHEA)
website: www.fchea.org

The FCHEA is the trade association devoted to commercializing fuel cells and hydrogen energy technologies. It encourages government support of fuel cell technology, including research and development.

National Renewable Energy Laboratory (NREL)
website: www.nrel.gov

The NREL maintains the National Fuel Cell Technology Evaluation Center, which gathers and manages data about state-of-the-art capabilities in fuel cell technology.

Renewable Energy Project Developer

What Does a Renewable Energy Project Developer Do?

A renewable energy project developer plays a crucial role in today's green energy economy. This person oversees all aspects of developing a renewable energy project, such as a large solar installation or wind farm. These responsibilities include identifying promising sites for projects; compiling resource data; acquiring land rights; securing grid interconnection rights and building permits; coordinating site studies, including geological, wildlife, and wetland analyses; and working with designers, engineers, and construction firms to complete the project. The developer often must work closely with financial experts to manage property tax agreements, negotiate leases, and apply for government subsidies. He or she must excel at multitasking and coordinating with a range of experts and skilled personnel. It is also essential that a renewable energy project developer stay current about the latest technologies in

At a Glance:
Renewable Energy Project Developer

Minimum Educational Requirements
Bachelor's degree

Personal Qualities
Detail oriented; flexible; industrious

Valuable Skills
Cost/benefit analysis; negotiating; coordinating

Working Conditions
Indoors in an office and travel to outdoor job sites

Salary Range
From $60,330 to $138,315

Future Job Outlook
Growth rate of 10 percent through 2024

solar power, wind energy, and related disciplines. Most project developers work at companies that specialize in one type of renewable energy, but some firms handle both wind and solar projects and even energy sources such as geothermal power.

Like any business venture, a renewable energy project faces significant risks. It also requires an enormous investment of time and money, and sometimes even political resources, to see the project through to completion. The first job for a renewable energy project developer is to identify a project that serves some fundamental need or interest. The project should be suitable to the energy economics of the chosen area and also fit into the area's policy consensus. The project should display clarity of purpose, with concrete goals. In early stages, the project developer also performs a fatal-flaw analysis, looking for any potentially disastrous factors that could scuttle the deal.

Screening and acquiring land for an energy project is one of the developer's most important jobs. Much time is spent at the computer using geographic information system software and other tools to investigate promising sites. Exhaustive research is necessary because land acquisition is always risky. The developer must be certain that the land for a proposed site is suitable for the project. Should problems arise that prevent the land from being used, the developer's company can lose money in property taxes and the opportunity cost of misdirecting the company's assets. For example, a large solar installation generally calls for land that is flat, with a slope of less than six degrees. The developer must also ascertain that the land is zoned correctly, allowing for a solar project. He or she must research the land deeds for any easements or restrictions that could interfere with development. Wetlands, wildlife, or other environmental factors must also be researched. The land must have convenient road access. Consideration of these factors begins at a broad level and then proceeds to more and more detailed analysis. The developer oversees this whole process of site acquisition and planning.

Next, the developer of a renewable energy project must determine that the project can be interconnected with the local power grid. Agreements with the public utilities commission may be necessary. Securing a power purchase agreement can be very complicated. One of the greatest risks is that the developer's new project will not get into the so-called interconnection queue—the line of generators seeking to connect to the transmission system. Yet the developer must try to ensure that a market exists for the power produced on-site from the first day of operation. This development phase also includes obtaining various permits, such as permits covering federal environmental regulations, electrical contracting permits, and building permits.

The renewable energy project developer must oversee the technology for the project, whether photovoltaic solar panels or wind turbines. This includes monitoring the project's engineering design, equipment selection, and building materials purchase. The developer must be closely involved in every aspect of building the project, from blueprint to construction. He or she must be able to integrate and lead a team of professionals, whether in finance, law, technology, or construction. Frequently, a project developer must monitor several projects at once, each at a different level of proposal or completion. Assuring that each project is proceeding according to schedule is a crucial responsibility for the project developer.

Developers of solar projects have to be well versed in current technology to ensure that each utility-scale solar plant can maximize its return on investment. For example, today, solar plants can be built to include sophisticated solar trackers. These motorized structures continually orient the photovoltaic panels toward the sun so they collect the greatest amount of direct sunlight throughout the day. The trackers can compensate for the slopes and irregular patches of the site's terrain. Tracker use tends to increase energy production at a solar plant by as much as 25 percent compared to installations with fixed tilt.

Likewise, in wind power projects, developers look for technology that makes the turbines more efficient and cost-effective. New offshore wind turbines work without a gearbox, making the entire drivetrain lighter, more compact, and less subject to wear. Even at lower wind speeds, the new turbines operate at greater levels of efficiency, delivering an energy yield that is 10 percent higher. Project developers are always on the lookout for innovations like these gearless turbines that can increase the profitability of a site. They are constantly reading technology magazines and industry journals for tips about possible game-changing breakthroughs.

A renewable energy project developer faces a challenging, competitive market that is always changing. He or she must strive to keep up with state renewable energy standards, incentive programs, tax credits, and fluctuations in energy prices. Ultimately, for all the concerns about improving the environment and providing clean energy, the developer must focus on the bottom line so that his or her company can make money and stay in business. "It's all about cost," says James Marlow, chief executive officer and founder of Atlanta-based Radiance Solar, on the Smart Electric Power Alliance website. "It's not about policy or optics or market: it's about cost."

How Do You Become a Renewable Energy Project Developer?

Education

To become a project developer in renewable energy, a student must have at least a bachelor's degree. The most helpful degree would be in engineering or in a scientific field such as chemistry or geology, with a minor in finance. Obtaining a master of business administration degree is also important in preparing a student for the economic challenges that a developer deals with every day. Above all, a renewable energy project developer must be versatile—part scientist, part politician, part financier. Therefore, his or her undergraduate and graduate education should include a variety of disciplines.

Students can also prepare for this occupation by taking advantage of programs outside of academia. In 2015 the International Renewable Energy Agency (IRENA) introduced a tool for prospective developers and energy planners called Project Navigator. It is a compilation of sources about how to pursue a renewable energy project, from proposal to completion. Project Navigator features case studies, expert advice, cost calculators, and other useful information. In an April 2015 press release Adnan Z. Amin, IRENA's director general, noted, "This new tool makes it easier for project developers to initiate, develop, fund, and complete renewable energy projects around the globe. It helps them overcome the barriers inherent in starting projects and, in doing so, facilitates the deployment of more renewable energy worldwide."

Training and Certification

Project developer positions generally require five or more years of experience in the renewable energy field. It is necessary for an aspiring developer to learn about all aspects of a renewable energy project, usually by way of company training with experienced professionals. When the person advances to the point of bringing his or her own projects to completion, he or she can attain certification by the Interstate Renewable Energy Council as a credentialed developer.

Skills and Personality

Professional skills for a renewable energy project developer include being capable of analyzing and identifying the best sites for projects; tracking state and local policies and market conditions for renewable energy; managing leases, permits, and factors related to grid interconnection and power sales; and integrating all aspects of a renewable energy project, from technical to political to financial.

A renewable energy project developer must be able to work in a fast-paced, ever-changing industry with confidence and verve. He or she should be self-motivated. The ability to multitask seamlessly is essential since the job calls for constantly switching gears to meet responsibilities and solve problems. A project developer must have excellent writing and speaking skills in order to describe a project and its needs in clear language. The person should be a fast learner with a strong sense of curiosity and an eye for detail. A developer must have excellent negotiating skills. He or she must be able to work easily with colleagues at all levels and show good leadership skills. The ability to analyze cost/benefit is another important advantage.

Employers

In general, renewable energy project developers work for private companies. These companies often specialize in one form of green energy.

Some project developers operate independently, serving as brokers who bring together the various pieces to launch a project. Developers may also work in government to pursue policy changes or regulations or to manage public-private partnerships in renewable energy.

Working Conditions

Renewable energy project developers must often work more than forty hours per week. Job requirements and emergencies frequently demand overtime work. Much of the developer's time is spent indoors at a computer or in meetings. However, he or she must also make regular trips to job sites.

Earnings

According to the employment website Indeed, renewable energy project developers make annual wages ranging from $60,330 to $138,315, with a median wage of $91,348. Those with added years of experience in the field, an invaluable asset, make the higher salaries.

What Is the Future Outlook for Renewable Energy Project Developers?

The prospects for job growth in renewable energy remain positive, and that includes prospects for project developers. In 2015 the US Congress extended the federal investment tax credit—a program that enables companies to pay lower taxes—for investments in solar and wind power through 2019, which represents a huge boost for the industry. This extension will allow the industry to continue its cost-cutting initiatives while working out innovative financing measures. With pricing for solar panels and wind turbines continuing to fall, these alternative sources of power will continue to gain ground in cost competition with fossil fuels. The current emphasis on reducing greenhouse gases and finding high-tech solutions to society's energy needs also promises healthy growth for the green energy field. Project developers should see job growth of up to 10 percent through 2024.

Find Out More

Association of Energy Engineers (AEE)
website: www.aeecenter.org

The AEE promotes the scientific and educational interests of engineers working in the energy industry and helps foster support for sustainable development projects.

International Renewable Energy Agency (IRENA)
website: www.irena.org

IRENA is an intergovernmental group that supports countries transitioning to a sustainable energy future. IRENA provides many tools for renewable energy project developers, including Project Navigator, a comprehensive look at how to manage an energy project from start to finish.

National Renewable Energy Laboratory (NREL)
website: www.nrel.gov

The NREL supports research, development, commercialization, and completion of renewable energy projects using the latest technologies.

US Department of Energy (DOE)
website: http://energy.gov

The DOE maintains programs on renewable energy project development and financing. Its website includes a breakdown of the steps in the project development process and how developers can coordinate their efforts with federal officials.

Interview with a Renewable Energy Project Developer

Mark Hannifan is the senior vice president of development for Tradewind Energy in Lenexa, Kansas. Tradewind is one of the largest wind and solar power development companies in the United States. He has over thirty-seven years of experience in the field of renewable energy, including positions with the National Renewable Energy Laboratory (NREL) in Golden, Colorado; a midwestern electric utility; and energy, environmental, and engineering consulting companies. He spoke with the author about his career.

Q: Why did you become a wind and solar power developer?

A: While I was attending college in the 1970s, the world experienced two oil crises, one in 1973 and the other in 1979. As I pursued undergraduate and master's degrees in architecture—and prompted by some sage advice from my petroleum geologist father—I began to explore how buildings could be designed to be more energy efficient and integrate solar systems to provide on-site power. I was then fortunate to begin my career fresh out of college with the nation's leading research laboratory, NREL, which conducts R&D [research and development] and market/policy analyses of solar, wind, geothermal, biofuels, and energy storage technologies. The technical and management experience gained at NREL and other professional positions—and a continued commitment to be involved in the deployment of sustainable power generation technologies—led me to my current position.

Q: Can you describe your typical workday?

A: I lead the formation of our company's solar development strategy and the overall management of development activities associated with our individual solar power projects. In that role I conduct analyses of the most promising market locations, identify suitable site opportunities in priority markets, and oversee project development tasks that include land acquisition, solar resource data collection, electrical interconnection modeling/studies, environmental site assessments, project permitting, and project engineering. There is considerable work conducted on the desktop in the office using geographic information systems and other engineering tools, but there is also significant work conducted on-site at the project locations, including geotechnical, wildlife, and wetland studies. Since we have approximately forty solar projects under development in over twenty states, there is a fair amount of travel involved.

Q: What do you find most rewarding about your job?

A: What I find most rewarding is knowing every wind power and solar power project our company develops and builds provides clean, affordable electricity for decades to come. I work with an incredible team of professionals from a number of disciplines, with many being recent graduates who are committed to fostering a transition from a dependency on fossil fuel–based power generation to a more balanced generation mix that includes increased reliance on wind and solar power.

Q: What personal qualities do you consider most valuable for this kind of work?

A: To be successful in this industry, one must 1) have a general if not intimate understanding of the big energy and environmental picture (e.g., how do different power technologies compare in terms of power price, what are the environmental characteristics of varying power technologies, what impact do energy/environmental policies and regulations and international geopolitics have on the industry); 2) be interested in how wind and solar power technologies work (e.g., how is sunlight converted to electricity, how many solar panels in a large solar project are needed to power say thirty thousand homes, etc.); 3) be able to convey with enthusiasm the positive attributes of wind and solar technologies to landowners, local/county officials, utility company personnel, and other interested project stakeholders; and 4) have a personal energy and drive and strong work ethic, as power development is hard, competitive, yet rewarding work.

Q: What advice do you have for students who might be interested in this career?

A: Whenever possible, take class work that covers energy technologies and environmental history/policies/regulations. Subscribe to a few of the many free digital renewable industry newsletters or forums so that you can be conversant in what is going on in the industry. Get involved in (or start) clubs focused on sustainability. Read popular, mainstream periodicals that cover energy/environmental-related technical, geopolitical, and market/financial topics (e.g., the *Economist*, *Wall Street Journal*, etc.). Plan to travel to and tour the exhibition hall at a national wind and/or solar conference where you will be blown away with the vast number of companies, energy technologies, and services on display, which would provide one-stop browsing of the range of job opportunities in the industry.

Other Jobs in Environmental and Energy Technology

Aquatic biologist
Building automation systems engineer
Carbon consultant
Certified energy auditor
Chemical engineer
Energy conservation coordinator
Environmental health and safety manager
Geophysical engineer
Geothermal operations manager

Green building engineer
Hydrographic surveyor
Nuclear engineer
Power optimization engineer
Resource conservation manager
Smart grid engineer
Soil conservation technician
Turf scientist
Utilities engineer
Wastewater engineer
Water resource engineer
Wetland specialist

Editor's Note: The US Department of Labor's Bureau of Labor Statistics provides information about hundreds of occupations. The agency's *Occupational Outlook Handbook* describes what these jobs entail, the work environment, education and skill requirements, pay, future outlook, and more. The *Occupational Outlook Handbook* may be accessed online at www.bls.gov/ooh.

Index

Note: Boldface page numbers indicate illustrations

Academy of Board Certified Environmental Professionals, 14
Accreditation Board of Engineering and Technology, 50
Agricultural Air Quality Task Force, 45
air pollution, effects of, 40
air quality forecasters
  basic information about, 40
  certification, 43
  earnings, 45
  educational requirements, 42–43
  employers, 43, 44
  information sources, 45–46
  job description, 40, 41–42, 44–45
  job outlook, 45
  on-the-job training, 43
  personal qualities/skills, 43–44
Air Quality Index (AQI), 41
Allen, Jason, 27
alternative energy. *See* green energy
American Geosciences Institute (AGI), 45–46
American Institute of Mining, Metallurgical, and Petroleum Engineers (AIME), 53
American Society for Engineering Education (ASEE), 59
American Society of Mechanical Engineers (ASME), 60
American Wind Energy Association (AWEA), 26, 32
Amin, Adnan Z., 7, 64–65
Association of Energy Engineers (AEE), 39, 67
Association of Environmental Studies and Sciences (AESS), 16–17
automobiles, electric-powered, 6, 54

Bakken shale formation (North Dakota), 49
biogas-powered fuel cells, 55
Bloom Energy, 55
Building Efficiency Initiative.org (website), 35

carpenters, job outlook, 7
certification
  air quality forecasters, 43
  energy consultants, 37
  environmental analysts, 14
  petroleum engineers, 50
  renewable energy project developers, 65
  solar PV installers, 21–22
  wind turbine technicians, 30
chemists, job outlook, 7
climate change analysts, 13
completions engineers, 48

continuing educational requirements, environmental analysts, 14

Deepwater Wind, 30
drilling engineers, 48

earnings
  air quality forecasters, 40, 45
  electricians, 8
  energy consultants, 33, 38
  engineers, 8
  environmental analysts, 10, 16
  environmental engineers, 8
  environmental scientists, 8
  environmental technicians, 8
  fuel cell engineers, 54, 59
  geoscientists, 8
  hydrologists, 8
  petroleum engineers, 47, 51–52
  power plant workers, 8
  renewable energy project developers, 61, 66
  solar PV installers, 8, 18, 23
  wind turbine technicians, 8, 26, 31
Ecological Society of America (ESA), 17
Ecotech Institute, 32
educational requirements
  air quality forecasters, 40, 42–43
  electricians, 8
  energy consultants, 33, 36
  engineers, 8
  environmental analysts, 10, 13–14
  environmental engineers, 8
  environmental scientists, 8
  environmental technicians, 8
  fuel cell engineers, 54, 56–57
  geoscientists, 8

hydrologists, 8
petroleum engineers, 47, 49–50
power plant workers, 8
renewable energy project developers, 61, 64–65
solar PV installers, 8, 18, 20
wind turbine technicians, 8, 26, 28
Electrical Training Alliance, 24
electricians
  earnings, 8
  educational requirements, 8
  job outlook, 7
  See also solar PV (photovoltaic) installers
electric-powered automobiles, 6, 54
electrolysis, 55
Electronics Technicians Association, International (ETA), 22, 24
energy consultants
  basic facts about, 33
  certification, 37
  earnings, 38
  educational requirements, 36
  employers, 37–38
  information sources, 39
  job description, 33–36, 38
  job outlook, 38
  personal qualities/skills, 37
Energy4Me (website), 48
energy technology career possibilities, 71
engineers
  earnings, 8
  educational requirements, 8
  job outlook, 7
environmental analysts
  basic facts about, 10
  certification, 14

continuing educational requirements, 14
earnings, 16
educational requirements, 13–14
employers, 15
information sources, 16–17
internships, 14
job description, 10–13, 12, 15–16
job outlook, 16
personal qualities/skills, 15
types of, 13
environmental engineers
earnings, 8
educational requirements, 8
environmental health specialists, 13
environmental scientists
earnings, 8
educational requirements, 8
environmental technicians
earnings, 8
educational requirements, 8
environmental technology career possibilities, 71

Fortune (magazine), 18
fossil fuels
natural gas wells in United States, 49
oil
reserves in US and Saudi Arabia, 47
reserves worldwide, 47–48
spill in Gulf of Mexico, 11
fracking, 49
Fuel Cell & Hydrogen Energy Association (FCHEA), 60
fuel cell engineers
basic facts about, 54
earnings, 59
educational requirements, 56–57
employers, 58
information sources, 59–60
job description, 54, 55–56, 58–59
job outlook, 7, 59
on-the-job training, 57
personal qualities/skills, 57–58
fuel cells
described, 54
pollution and, 54, 55
uses for, 55

gas chromatography, 12
General Motors, 58
geographic information system (GIS) software, 15, 41–42, 62
geologists, job outlook, 7
geoscientists
earnings, 8
educational requirements, 8
job outlook, 7
geostationary satellites, 41
government
incentives
importance of, 7
and job outlook for solar PV installers, 24
tax credits for solar and wind power, 66
jobs for
air quality forecasters, 44
environmental analysts, 11, 13, 15
fuel cell engineers, 58
renewable energy project developers, 66
regulations, 11
green energy
career possibilities, 71
current increase in job growth, 7
factors for project developers to

consider, 62–63
job outlook, 7
making fuel cells, 55
types of jobs, 9
ground-level ozone, 41
Gulf of Mexico, oil spill in, 11

Hannifan, Mark, 68–70
homes of future, 6
hydraulic fracturing, 49
hydrogen, 54, 55
hydrologists
    earnings, 8
    educational requirements, 8

Ikea, 55
Independent Energy Consultants
    (IEC), 39
Independent Energy Consultants
    (website), 37
industrial ecologists, 13
Inside Jobs (website), 54
Institute of Environmental
    Management & Assessment, 9
Institute of Hazardous Materials
    Management, 14
interconnection queue, described,
    63
International Renewable Energy
    Agency (IRENA)
    about, 67
    contact information, 67
    increase in green energy jobs
        (2015), 7
    project development tool, 64–65
International Society for Industrial
    Ecology (ISIE), 17
Internet of Things and saving
    energy, 34–35
internships, 14

Interstate Renewable Energy
    Council, 65

job descriptions. See working
    conditions
job outlook
    air quality forecasters, 40, 45
    carpenters, 7
    chemists, 7
    electricians, 7
    energy consultants, 33, 38
    engineers, 7
    environmental analysts, 10, 16
    forecast for 2030, 7
    fuel cell engineers, 54, 59
    geologists, 7
    geoscientists, 7
    increase in green energy jobs
        (2015), 7
    materials scientists, 7
    petroleum engineers, 47, 52
    renewable energy project
        developers, 61, 66
    solar PV installers, 18, 24
    in wind turbine industry, 27
    wind turbine technicians, 26,
        31–32
job satisfaction, 9

Leadership in Energy and
    Environmental Design
    certification programs, 37, 39

Marcellus shale formation
    (Pennsylvania), 49
Marlow, James, 64
mass spectrometry, 12
materials scientists, job outlook, 7
Meteorological Society's Certified
    Consulting Meteorologist

(CCM) Program, 43
meteorologists, 40, 41
Musk, Elon, 6

National Association of
  Environmental Professionals
  (NAEP), 17
National Center for Construction
  Education and Research
  (NCCER), 24–25
National Energy Education
  Development project, 56–57
National Oceanic and Atmospheric
  Administration (NOAA), 44, 46
National Park Service, 44
National Renewable Energy
  Laboratory (NREL), 60, 67
National Society of Professional
  Engineers (NSPE), 53
National Weather Service, 43
natural gas wells in United States,
  49
North American Board of Certified
  Energy Practitioners (NABCEP),
  21–22, 25
nuclear engineers
  earnings, 8
  educational requirements, 8
nuclear technicians
  earnings, 8
  educational requirements, 8

Occupational Outlook Handbook
  (Bureau of Labor Statistics), 71
Occupational Safety & Health
  Administration, 22
offshore wind turbines, 30, 63
oil
  reserves in US and Saudi Arabia,
    47

reserves worldwide, 47–48
spill in Gulf of Mexico, 11
on-the-job training
  air quality forecasters, 43
  fuel cell engineers, 57
  renewable energy project
    developers, 65
  solar PV installers, 20
  wind turbine technicians, 28–29

PayScale (website), 38
personal qualities/skills
  air quality forecasters, 40, 43–44
  energy consultants, 33, 37
  environmental analysts, 10, 15
  fuel cell engineers, 54, 57–58
  petroleum engineers, 47, 50–51
  renewable energy project
    developers, 61, 65, 69–70
  solar PV installers, 18, 22, 23
  wind turbine technicians, 26, 30
petroleum engineers
  basic facts about, 47
  certification, 50
  earnings, 51–52
  educational requirements, 49–50
  employers, 51
  information sources, 53
  job description, 47, 48–49, 51
  job outlook, 52
  personal qualities/skills, 50–51
pollutants, identifying, 12
polymer electrolyte membrane fuel
  cells, 56
power plant workers
  earnings, 8
  educational requirements, 8
production engineers, 48
Project Navigator, 64–65

Read, Tobias, 52
renewable energy. *See* green energy
renewable energy project developers
  basic facts about, 61
  certification, 65
  earnings, 66
  educational requirements, 64–65
  employers, 65–66
  information sources, 67
  job description, 61–64, 66, 69
  job outlook, 66
  on-the-job training, 65
  personal qualities/skills, 65, 69–70
reservoir engineers, 48
reservoirs (of oil and gas),
    described, 48
Riptide, 35
Roof Integrated Solar Energy, 22
Rystad Energy, 47–48

satellites, 41
Saudi Arabia, oil reserves in, 47
Sellers, Fred, 31
Sinclair, Ken, 35
site restoration planners, 13
Society of Petroleum Engineers
    (SPE), 50, 53
SolarCity, 6
solar energy
  cost of, 18
  factors for project developers to
    consider, 62–63
  tax credits, 66
solar PV (photovoltaic) installers
  basic facts about, 18
  certification, 21–22
  earnings, 8, 23
  educational requirements, 8, 20
  employers, 22–23
  information sources, 24–25

job description, 18–20, 21, 23
job outlook, 24
on-the-job training, 20
personal qualities/skills, 22, 23
Solar Ready Vets, 23
solar trackers, described, 63
solid oxide fuel cell technology, 55
Stover, Nic, 9
subsurface engineers, 48
Summit Energy, 39

tariffs, defined, 34
Tesla Motors, 6
Timmer, John, 27
Tradewind Energy, 68

Underwood, Kristin, 18–19, 20
United States
  natural gas wells, 49
  number of wind turbines
    operating, 26
  oil reserves, 47
  See also government; specific
    agencies; specific departments
US Bureau of Labor Statistics
    (BLS)
  earnings of
    air quality forecasters, 45
    environmental analysts, 16
    petroleum engineers, 51–52
    solar PV installers, 23
    wind turbine technicians, 31
  job outlook for
    air quality forecasters, 45
    consulting services, 38
    environmental analysts, 16
    petroleum engineers, 52
    solar PV installers, 24
    wind turbine technicians,
      31–32

Occupational Outlook Handbook, 71

types of employers of solar PV installers, 22–23

types of employers of wind turbine technicians, 30

US Department of Defense, 23

US Department of Energy (DOE), 23

  contact information, 67

  employment of fuel cell engineers by, 58

  information about renewable energy project development and financing, 67

  National Energy Education Development project, 56–57

  prediction of global increase in fuel cell technology, 59

  wind power predictions

    energy cost savings, 26–27

    job outlook in wind turbine industry, 27

US Environmental Protection Agency (EPA), 41, 44

US Green Building Council (USGBC), 37, 39

US veterans, jobs for solar PV installers, 23

Walgreens and energy savings, 35

weather forecasts, 40

wildcat firms, 51

Wind Energy Foundation, 32

Windpower Engineering & Development (website), 31

Wind Systems (online magazine), 27

windtech. *See* wind turbine technicians

wind turbines

  efficiency, 63

  location of future, 30

  number operating in US, 26

  tax credits, 66

wind turbine technicians

  basic facts about, 26

  certification, 30

  earnings, 8, 31

  educational requirements, 8, 28

  employers, 30

  information sources, 32

  job description, 26, 27, 29, 31

  job outlook, 31–32

  on-the-job training, 28–29

  personal qualities/skills, 30

WindTurbineTechnicians.net, 32

Wind Vision Report (DOE), 26–27

working conditions

  air quality forecasters, 40, 41–42, 44–45

  energy consultants, 33, 38

  environmental analysts, 10–13, 12, 15–16

  fuel cell engineers, 54, 55–56, 58–59

  petroleum engineers, 47, 48–49, 51

  renewable energy project developers, 61–64, 66, 69

  solar PV installers, 18–20, 21, 23

  wind turbine technicians, 26, 27, 29, 31

World Meteorological Organization (WMO), 46

Wyle Laboratories, 15

Picture Credits

About the Author

John Allen is a writer living in Oklahoma City.